Published in 2009
by Igloo Books Ltd
Cottage Farm
Sywell
NN6 0BJ

www.igloo-books.com

10 9 8 7 6 5 4 3 2 1

ISBN: 978-1-84817-518-1

Printed and manufactured in China

THE
WISHING
WELL

Edgar J. Hyde

Contents

Waterwheel Farm   4
Tom's Secret   7
A New School   11
The Well Talks Back   16
A Second Day at School   20
Tom Escapes   28
A Strange Event   32
The Flour Fight   35
A Troublesome Incident   40
An Old Tale   45
Tom Makes a Wish   51
George's Lesson   56
The Spirit of the Well   60
The Water Queen   65
Spite Seeks Revenge   71
Out of Control   80
A Helpful Priest   86
The Mystery of the Barn   91
A Spell Goes Wrong   95
A Final Showdown   103

Chapter 1:

Waterwheel Farm

Tom stared out of the back bedroom window. Downstairs, he could hear his Mom shouting to his Dad. She sounded happy and excited. He let out a big sigh. Mom always got everything the way that she wanted, sometimes she was really awful to live with. This was one of those times. He could hear her really annoying voice ringing in his head...

"Now Tom," she had said, "try not to be difficult, everyone has to make changes sometimes and get used to rules..."

Tom had not replied to this. It wasn't exactly a question. Besides, Mom very rarely left room for other people to say what they felt.

"... there will be lots of exciting things for you to do, when I was a little girl I never had half of the toys that you have, Aunt Margaret and I had to make do with an old cardboard box, yes, I know you don't believe me, you probably can't even imagine it..."

This was the point when Tom drowned Mom out of his head. He had heard this speech at least a thousand times. If he was in the mood when

The Wishing Well

he actually liked Mom, he perhaps might have marvelled at the way she seemed to repeat this word for word every time, or that she didn't seem to have to breathe like the rest of the human race. Mom just couldn't understand that Tom wasn't a child any more. He was fourteen and didn't need to be babied.

The problem was that they had recently moved to a new house. When the car had swung into the long drive, Tom had been excited by the thought of finding places to disappear to where Mom couldn't find him. But Mom had spoilt his fun by listing loads of places that he was forbidden to go to in case he had an accident. There were places on the farm that were dangerous. Tom thought Mom was being silly and overprotective.

The new house was a large rambling building, with strange sticky-out bits that dad had called awnings. It sat in the middle of an old courtyard, and had an old sign that said "Waterwheel Farm". Tom had never lived in a house that had a name before. It had been a working farm but the farmer had sold off most of the land to nearby farmers and emigrated to Australia. It had been Mom's dream to live here. She had grown up not far from here and she had always loved it, so when she saw it was up for sale, well... Mom always got her own way.

Creepers

He could hear Mom clattering about in the kitchen. He slipped off the chair and ran downstairs two at a time. He opened the front door and stared out. A large barn was opposite the front of the house. There was a loud squeaking noise as a rusty old weather vane on top of the barn spun round in the wind. Tom closed the door quietly behind him and slipped outside.

Chapter 2:

Tom's Secret

What was left of the old courtyard curved around the house and led to a lane. Most of the path had long disappeared but if you concentrated really hard you could trace it for quite a while before it disappeared completely. Tom had been working on the path for a while to try and discover where exactly it led to.

He had managed to follow it to a line of trees and then had lost it. Today he found a little more. A large boulder sat across his way. He pulled hard at it but couldn't shift it. He looked around and saw a large branch that had fallen off one of the trees. He dragged it over to the boulder and with the heel of his boot dug out a groove to push the branch into. At first he didn't think it was going to budge, then with one huge shove it toppled over, revealing a large slab of the path.

Tom dragged away the grass that covered the path and took up his trail. The path wound into the small forest. The trees towered above him making him feel small. The sun streaked through the large trees.

Creepers

Tom thought it was just like being in his room at night when he read with a flashlight under his bedclothes. The large branches shielded the main glow of the sun just allowing it to peek through the spaces.

Suddenly, in the distance he saw a strange shape. It was perfectly round and had a shiny little roof. At first he thought it was a Wendy house. As he drew nearer to the shape he realised that it was a well. It stuck out of the earth in the most peculiar way. It was a strange place for a well to be, so far from the house. Even stranger – it didn't look as old as the rest of the buildings. It looked almost as though it had been built yesterday. A shiny new L-shaped handle stuck out of the side. Tom followed the shape of the handle as it stretched across the large gaping hole. In the middle of its bar was a thick rope, which was tied securely to a large wooden bucket. He leaned over the side to see inside it. The hole loomed beneath him and seemed to go on for miles. He shouted into it.

"Hey!"

His voice came back and sounded small and silly. He giggled into the space: "Ha-ha-ha!"

Again, the echo returned like a tiny voice. He decided to lower the bucket into the well. Placing

The Wishing Well

both hands on the handle he used all his strength to turn it, but he needn't have bothered, the handle moved easily and the force of Tom pushing sent the pail rattling down the shaft, clattering off the stone sides. Eventually there was an almighty splash as the bucket hit the water and the handle juddered to a halt. He needed all his strength to pull the bucket up. It was full of water and very heavy. When it arrived he drank some of the water, which felt cool and refreshing.

Tom looked around him and saw another boulder. He dragged it over to the well. Using all his strength he heaved the boulder over the side into the well. He began to wander around looking for stones and throwing them in. Each time he threw something in he would listen carefully to see how long it took before it landed. He started to time them, counting the seconds so that he could guess how deep it was. After a while anything he could find went into the well – the top of a rusty old spade, an old shoe, a can of juice.

"TOOOMMM!!!"

Tom had forgotten all about Mom, Dad – in fact, everything. He turned quickly and began to run back the way he had come. This was going to be his special place and he didn't want anyone to know where it was. He reached the edge of the trees just as Mom released another shrill "TOM!" He ran along the path in time to catch Mom coming around the side of the house.

"Where have you been Tom? I was beginning to worry, look at the state of you, my goodness your dinner is nearly cold, now hurry up and get inside and take those clothes off, they're covered in..."

Tom grunted in Mom's direction and quickly ran into the house smiling. His secret was safe.

Chapter 3:

A New School

Today was Monday. Not just any Monday but the most horrible Monday in the world. It was Tom's first day at his new school. He shuffled uncomfortably inside the new clothes that Mom had insisted he wear. He stared out of the window and the world stared back. What was the point of school anyway? He knew it wouldn't be like his old school and he knew he wouldn't find anyone like his old friends.

Dad called upstairs to say it was time to go and Tom dragged his schoolbag across the floor towards the bedroom door. He made sure that his bag banged off every step down the stairway and gave a huge sigh when he reached the bottom.

"Come on Tom, cheer up," said Dad "it's not the end of the world."

Dad didn't understand, no-one did.

The journey to the local high school was not long enough, thought Tom. It was in the nearby town called Rosehill. Rosehill School sounded like a nice place but it didn't look nice. Before long he

Creepers

stood in a corridor of the big noisy school. Children everywhere seemed to be in a hurry, shouting each other's names and pushing each other about. The loud bell rang and the chaos that was in front of him multiplied. There was a rush of pupils running to classes shouting that they'd see each other at break. Tom felt alone.

Dad introduced him to the headmaster, gave him a smile and then left. The headmaster told Tom to follow him and took him up some stairs and into a large classroom. There was silence in the class as the head entered. Tom felt his face go red as everyone's eyes were upon him. The head introduced him to the teacher and then left.

"Everyone, this is Tom Walker, he's new to the school and I want you to make him welcome. Sit here Tom and I'll give you a timetable."

Tom's face remained red. He daren't look round because he knew everyone was looking at him. He felt like an alien.

"Harry, I want you to show Tom around for the first week 'till he's settled."

A tall boy with dark curly hair and dressed in school uniform stood up.

"Aw Miss, why me?"

The teacher glared at him and Harry sat down.

The Wishing Well

The morning seemed endless as Harry reluctantly dragged Tom around with him. He barely spoke and Tom felt miserable. Lunchtime was worse as Harry deserted Tom in a large hall that was bustling with children with eager faces, trying to meet up with their friends – talking, laughing and shouting as loud as they could. Tom decided not to have lunch and went out into the playground.

There were some boys playing football in the corner. They didn't notice him. Tom wandered around looking for something, anything to make him feel better. He walked round the corner and saw a group of boys huddled over something, laughing.

Tom went over to see what they were doing. One of the boys had a stick and was poking something. The other boys seemed to be encouraging him. All Tom could see was the top of a bucket. Then he heard the most awful noise; a high pitched squeal that came from an animal. Something in him made him start running towards the gang, he felt scared, but he knew he had to keep running. Tom's instinct had been right because there in the middle of the boys was a squirrel, trapped in the bucket while the boys cruelly taunted it.

Tom leapt on top of the boy with the stick and punched him in the eye. The boy reeled backwards knocking over the bucket and the squirrel ran up the nearest tree. All the boys stood still and looked straight at Tom. The boy he knocked over stood up and said:

"I'll get you for that Walker. "

Tom stood his ground but felt strangely alone: no-one moved. The boys began to edge towards him, until they eventually surrounded him. The boy who spoke began to push him. The rest soon joined in and Tom was shoved to the ground, colliding with the upturned bucket. He heard his jacket rip. A man's voice rang out over the playground:

"What's going on?"

The boys all moved away as Tom struggled to his feet.

"I asked you a question, Simpson?"

Simpson was the boy who had been torturing the squirrel.

"Nothing sir, we were playing a game and Walker fell on the bucket."

The teacher looked round at the faces in the group. Not recognizing Tom's face he said:

"You must be new here, is this true?"

Tom looked at the ground and nodded.

At that moment the bell rang. The teacher looked at everyone suspiciously.

The Wishing Well

"Well", he said "Get to your classes."

He watched them all walk back towards the building. As they entered, Simpson looked over at Tom and mouthed the word "later".

Chapter 4:
The Well Talks Back

When the bell went at the end of his first day at school, Tom felt an incredible sense of relief. The children all ran out of the classrooms and headed for the school gates. Tom was one of the last people to come out of the building. He had made no friends and the incident with the squirrel had left him convinced that he was definitely not going to like this school. He thought he ought to put his jacket in his bag so that Mom didn't get upset about the tear in it. He could see a crowd of boys at the school gates and he began to feel nervous. He was hoping it wasn't the same boys from lunchtime, but as he got nearer he could here them say:

"Here he comes."

The boys all turned to face him and barred his way through the gates. At that point, a car pulled up behind them and Tom saw his Dad getting out. Dad waved and Tom waved back. The gang looked surprised and thought that Tom was waving at them. Dad spoke:

"Hi Tom, how was your first day?"

The Wishing Well

The boys were startled and shuffled aside to let Tom through. Dad got back in the car and as Tom went around to get into the passenger seat he heard the boys laughing. He knew they were laughing at him but he ignored them and got in the car.

Dad repeated his question, and Tom said that it was "OK".

"Just 'OK'? Did you make any new friends?", Tom answered "no", and Dad told him that it was first day nerves and that he probably would tomorrow. Tom stared out of the window as the car made towards home. Dad's last remark left him feeling quite sick and he dreaded the thought of another day at school.

When they got home, Tom asked if he could go outside. Mom told him dinner wouldn't be long but that he could go out for a little while. Tom changed out of his school clothes and ran down the stairs, out the front door and made straight for the well. When he got there he leaned over the side and let out a long scream. The scream echoed back and almost frightened him. Tom thought: "I hate those boys, I hate those boys." He then said it out loud into the well:

"I hate those boys!"

The well shouted it straight back at him. Tom

laughed, it was as though the well hated those boys too.

"Stupid, stupid boys!" he shouted.

The well agreed with him.

"Torturing that little squirrel, what bullies."

The well agreed with him again.

Tom exhausted himself shouting exactly what he thought of those boys into the well. He sat down and leaned against its stone wall, and thought about tomorrow and how he would have to go back to the school. He immediately stood up and shouted into the well again.

"Stupid, stupid school."

The well echoed back his remark, like a close friend who agrees with everything you think. Tom thought about Mom and Dad bringing him to this place and shouted into the well:

"Stupid Mom and Dad"

The word Dad seemed to ring out for a long time before it died away.

"TOOOMMM"

Mom's voice rang out loud and clear as if in answer to the echo of the well – Tom leapt up and ran towards the house.

He opened the kitchen door in time to see Mom placing his meal on the table.

The Wishing Well

The kitchen was warm and his parents bustled about with their usual routine as Tom closed the door behind him and sat down to join them.

Chapter 5:

A Second Day at School

When Mom came in to tell Tom it was time to get up the next morning, Tom groaned and with his feeblest voice said:

"Mom I don't feel well, I think I've got a sore throat."

Mom gave Tom the look of a woman who had been there, seen it and done it. She raised an eyebrow – she often did this when she was suspicious of what was going on. Tom was insistent.

"No, really, Mom, I think I've got a temperature, I feel hot and sweaty."

Mom walked across the bedroom floor and placed her hand on his forehead.

"You don't feel too hot to me" she said. Tom looked at her pleadingly. Sometimes that worked. Mom sat down on the edge of the bed and looked into Tom's face. "Tom, is there something you want to tell me? Is it your new school?"

Tom hadn't expected Mom to ask him this, and he hesitated before answering. Should he tell her about the squirrel, or would that make everything worse? Mom might want to come up to the school, and if she thought he was being bullied she might even begin to collect him every day and that would be really embarrassing. Tom decided to make a remarkable recovery.

"Actually Mom, I don't feel so bad after all, I think I'll be OK."

Mom raised her eyebrow again. Tom smiled at her nervously and leapt out of the bed and headed for the bathroom.

"Tom," Mom said, "if there's anything bothering you, you know you can talk to me don't you?"

Tom thought: "Me and my big mouth, now I've got to throw Mom off the scent."

"Mom, stop going on," he sighed, as he slammed the bathroom door.

He could hear Mom going down the stairs and he breathed a sigh of relief. "Phew, close one."

Over breakfast Mom kept giving him strange looks, the kind that Moms give when they are about to start fussing over you and they think that you can't cope with being out of their protection. Tom could have kicked himself.

He tried to make himself almost invisible so that he didn't draw any more attention to himself than was necessary and almost ran over Dad when he suggested it was time for them to go.

"What on earth is wrong with that boy?" he heard Dad remark to Mom.

"Adolescence dear," she had replied, in a sort of tired voice. They gave each other a knowing look and Dad got into the car. Tom hated that knowing look. It was something adults always did to exclude children. Tom decided not to mention anything else to Mom or Dad to avoid any more knowing looks.

The bell rang just as the car pulled up at the gates. Tom felt his heart sink, and he began to get out of the car slowly. Dad told him to hurry up as he was making him late for work, then he reminded Tom that today he would have to start getting the bus home, and did Tom remember where the bus stop was, and what number it was, and did Tom have enough money? Tom felt very irritated and answered all Dad's questions before stomping off in a bad mood.

The morning's classes were really boring. Tom had double chemistry in the morning and he stared out of the window for most of the time. Just when he thought it couldn't get any worse his timetable showed him that he had gym class – Tom hadn't brought his sports kit. There was a ten minute break before the lesson started and Tom sat down on a small bench outside. Everywhere he looked there were children talking and laughing and Tom tried to listen to the conversation of two girls who stood nearby. They were talking about the latest music in the charts and how much they liked it. Tom groaned inside that he hated that kind of music. A voice behind him made him turn around.

"You're the new boy aren't you?"

A tall boy who looked about the same age as Tom stood before him. Tom had seen him in classes yesterday.

"My name's David"

Tom said hello and told him his name. David asked Tom where he was from and where he lived now.

"Waterwheel Farm"

When Tom said the name of the farm, David looked at him with wide eyes.

"Tom, that farm's really exciting, there's supposed to be a haunted forest over there."

At that moment the bell rang and David said that he'd see Tom later. Tom felt excited at this news, he would have to go and search for it. His excitement had made him forget that he was now going to the gymhall. He quickly ran over to the hall and pushed open one of the large swinging doors that led to the room. There were a lot of children hurrying to the end of the hall where Tom could see teachers in tracksuit bottoms with whistles around their necks beckoning to them to go into two rooms.

"Boys to the left, girls to the right," bellowed one teacher with a large moustache. They were going into changing rooms. A small round woman with a whistle around her neck beckoned Tom over. She introduced herself as Miss Emslie and Tom explained that he had no kit.

"Easily sorted," she replied in a brusque voice and she took Tom to a small store room that was nearby.

She bent over a large box and began to rummage inside. When she stood up she had an old pair of shorts, a washed out T-shirt and an old pair of trainers. She pushed them at him and sent him into the changing room.

The room was filled with boys of all shapes and sizes wriggling out of their clothes and climbing into sports gear. Tom felt the hot flush of his face as he found a quiet corner to change in. There was a teacher with a moustache calling for the boys to hurry up and return to the hall so that he could take a register.

When Tom came out the boys all stood in a long line as the teacher called their names.

The Wishing Well

"Steve Simpson."

"Here sir."

Tom looked up to see the boy who had been torturing the squirrel.

"George Foster."

Tom recognized another boy from the incident.

"Billy Watson."

Tom felt uncomfortable. The boys hadn't noticed him until Miss Emslie pointed him out to the teacher with the moustache who wrote his name down. A snigger went through the group as they looked at the clothes he was wearing. The teacher quickly explained that today they were going to play basketball and split the boys into two groups before he positioned them on the court.

Tom was to remain near the net and shadow George Foster. The teacher with the moustache puffed into his whistle and the game began. The boys enthusiastically called out to each other as the ball was passed from one end of the court to the other. One boy would be running with it then another would manage to get it from him and they would run in the other direction.

"Steve, to me, to me!"

A small boy who could run fast waved frantically at Simpson who threw the ball in his direction.

Creepers

Another boy in Tom's team managed to reach it before the small boy could and it quickly began to weave its way towards Tom.

George Foster was darting in front of Tom and blocking his view of the ball. Tom turned sharply in time to see the ball flying towards him. He thought he could reach it and leapt into the air to catch it. Suddenly he felt his feet give out underneath him and he landed on the floor with a loud crack. The whistle blew and the teacher with the moustache shouted:

"Simpson what are you doing at that end of the court? Get to the other end immediately."

Tom looked up to see Simpson grinning at him as he walked to the end of the court. The whistle blew and the game started again.

The ball bounced and flew at all angles as the boys tried to outwit each other. One boy was hit full in the face as he tried to catch the ball. Then Tom's opportunity came again. The ball was being bounced up the court in his direction. He managed to dodge George Foster and caught the ball firmly in his arms. Tom began to run up the court towards the net. He looked firmly at his destination and with a leap hurled the ball through the air towards the net. A few of the taller boys in the other team tried

The Wishing Well

to stop its flight, but the ball slapped hard against the backboard before sliding down into the gaping net. The boys in Tom's team let out a huge cheer. Tom grinned looking around at his fellow team and caught sight of Simpson's scowl. The teacher blew his whistle and told the boys it was time to shower and change.

The chatter in the changing room was loud as the boys shouted happily to each other. People were now interested in Tom and wanted to know where he was from and where he lived. Tom answered their questions and found out a few things about them. The bell rang and they all began to trickle out of the room to go to their next class. Tom turned at the door of the changing room to check that he hadn't left anything behind. Simpson and his cronies stood together scowling at him. Tom turned and walked into the throng of boys ahead of him.

Chapter 6:

Tom Escapes

The rest of the day went well and when the bell rang at the end of the day Tom felt a lot happier. He had managed to avoid Simpson and his friends and so had forgotten all about them. He stood for a moment at the school gates to check in which direction he should head and then began the walk to the bus stop. The route to the bus stop followed an old canal path, at the end of which he was to cross a bridge that would lead him to the edge of the town.

Tom walked absent-mindedly along the path, whistling. Up ahead he could see that some trees had fallen onto the path and a large trunk blocked his way. The trunk looked easy enough to climb over and Tom hitched his bag over his shoulder as he began to climb up. Half way over, his jumper caught on to a jagged piece of bough that was sticking out of the trunk. Tom tried to pull his jumper but the wool had caught fast. Just then Tom felt something hit him hard on the back of the ear.

The blow stung and Tom lifted his hand up to the back of his head to feel the cut. When his hand came back it was covered in blood. Tom looked around but could see no-one. He pulled furiously at his jumper to try and release it but it was twisted on to the tree. Another missile hit him hard in the middle of his forehead. Tom heard voices laughing. Then a mocking voice said:

"You're nothing but a country bumpkin."

Tom recognized Simpson's voice immediately and began frantically to pull at his jumper. The jumper ripped and Tom leapt over the other side of the trunk just as another stone whistled past his ear.

Tom began to run as the boys gave chase. Up ahead he could see the bridge that he must cross. The boys chased him down the canal path shouting horrible names and throwing stones at him. Tom ran over the bridge wincing with the sting of the cut behind his ear. As he crossed the bridge he could see the bus stop at the top of the road.

There was a queue of about five adults at the bus stop and in the distance he could see his bus turning the corner and heading toward the stop. The boys were still running after him. Tom's side began to ache as he ran up the road. The stitch was slowing him down. The bus had pulled up at the stop and the people were getting on. Tom ran as fast as he could. The last passenger was getting on the bus and Tom felt his heart sink as he realized that he was going to miss it.

The last passenger's shopping bag burst and she had to pick her shopping up.

"Yes!" thought Tom, "I can make it."

A woman and a small child in a pushchair suddenly appeared in front of him and Tom lost his balance. He managed to stop himself falling over and reached the stop just as the bus revved its engine and began to pull away.

"Stop, wait for me," Tom shouted.

The driver saw Tom in the long mirror on the side of the bus and slowed down with a squeal. The old doors squeaked open and Tom leapt on. He staggered to the back of the bus in time to see his pursuers reach the bus stop and glare breathlessly after their prey. Tom fell into his seat and tried to catch his breath.

When he arrived home, he ran straight up the stairs to the bathroom so as to avoid Mom. Tom looked in the mirror and saw what he suspected. A bruise the size of an egg was forming in the middle of his forehead. He filled the sink with water and placed a flannel on his head. He then tried to clean up the cut on his ear as best he could. Tom dried his face on the towel that hung on the rail beside the

The Wishing Well

sink and looked into the mirror again. The bruise was turning purple.

He went downstairs to face Mom. As he pushed open the kitchen door he saw that the room was empty. On the middle of the kitchen table leaning against an empty milk carton was a note. Mom had gone to the supermarket but would be back soon. Tom decided that he take a walk to the well to clear his aching head.

When he arrived at the well, Tom leaned over the side and stared into the hole. Very slowly and deliberately he spoke into it:

"I hate Steve Simpson, I wish he could be taught a lesson."

His voice had been so low that the well merely rumbled back what he had said. Tom rested his head into his hands and sighed.

Chapter 7:

A Strange Event

Steve Simpson lived in a small house in Rosewell. He had two much older brothers who he didn't get on with. His mother was a fierce woman. His father was a large grim-looking man who spent most of his time away from home to avoid arguing with his wife. Whenever Steve came home he got in a row. Either with his brothers who accused him of touching their things or his Mom who was always going on about the state of his room, or his dad who thought children should be seen and not heard.

After chasing Tom up the road, Steve and his friends had gone for chips. The running had made Steve sweaty and the chips had made him feel greasy so he had gone home to wash. Steve locked the bathroom door behind him and put the plug in the sink. He turned on the hot and cold taps and began to wash his face and hands. The soap went into his eyes and began to sting. Steve screwed his face up and stretched his arms out to feel for the towel that hung nearby. There was no towel there. He squinted against the sting in his eyes and saw a dirty towel

The Wishing Well

lying on the bathroom floor.

He knelt down on the floor and rubbed his face with the towel. Just then a drop of water hit him on the back of the head. Water was still running in the sink. Steve stood up in time to see water overflowing onto the floor. He turned the faucet, but it wouldn't move. He tried to wrap the dirty towel around it to give him more power but it still wouldn't move. Steve pulled at the plug and the chain came off it. The plug was stuck in the drain.

He looked around the room for something to help him. There was nothing there that he could see. Then he had a brainwave. If he turned on the bath that would stem some of the flow from the sink. He leant across the tub and turned the hot and cold water on. The water gushed into the empty bath but the sink still remained the same. Steve looked into the bath which had now begun to fill up. The drain appeared to be blocked.

He tried to turn off the bath water but it continued to flow. He was beginning to panic. His trainers had begun to squelch across the lino as the floor was becoming waterlogged. The bath began to spill water over its sides. Steve bent down and tried to mop up the water with a towel and squeeze it into the toilet. The towel quickly became soaked and it made little difference. Just then, Steve heard a shout from downstairs.

"THERE'S WATER COMING THROUGH THE CEILING."

Steve's heart began to beat fast as he heard his mother running up the stairs.

"STEPHEN, OPEN THIS DOOR AT ONCE YOUNG MAN."

His mother didn't sound as though she was prepared to be reasonable. Steve opened the door and stared into his mother's face which was red from screaming and revealed two large flaring nostrils. His mother swiped at him and he ducked.

"Mom, it's the water, I can't turn it off!" Steve wailed. His mother's fluffy slippers slapped across the now sodden bathroom floor. She leant across the sink and turned off the water with ease. Steve edged nearer the open bathroom door. His mother leant across the bath and repeated what she had done at the sink. She turned and scowled at Steve. Through gritted teeth she said:

"Get this mess cleaned up now!"

With that remark she stormed out of the bathroom taking a small wave of water with her. Steve stood still, his mouth wide open as he stared at the mess with disbelief.

Chapter 8:

The Flour Fight

Mom was going on and on about the bruise on Tom's forehead. He had told her that he had tripped and fallen and she was now giving a long speech about Tom's lack of common sense and how he never paid enough attention to where he was putting his enormous feet. They were sitting at breakfast and Tom was saying nothing. He was just imagining ways to stop her talking. This made the whole lecture bearable. He thought of his smelliest socks stuffed into her mouth and a smile crept across his face.

"It's not funny Tom," she scolded. "One day you'll have a serious accident if you're not careful."

Tom nodded, he knew better than to interrupt her when she was in this mood. Dad said it was time to go and Tom leapt up, spilling his half empty bowl of cereal. Mom's eyebrow shot into the air. She had that look on her face which said triumphantly "See, what did I tell you?" Tom made an attempt to clean up the mess but Mom shooed him out of the kitchen and did it herself.

Creepers

He thought he was going to have an easy ride to school, but Dad continued where Mom had left off. Tom was relieved to see the school looming up ahead. Dad had hardly pressed the brake before Tom was out of the car and running towards the school gates.

The first class was a cooking class. The pupils were paired off and each pair had their own cooker. Tom had been paired off with David, the boy he had met in the playground. Billy Watson and George Foster were at the next cooker. A large cheery woman with rosy cheeks called Mrs Johnston was the teacher of the class. She looked like the sort of person who spent a lot of her time baking, and very probably eating, cakes.

Mrs Johnston said they were going to make a cheese sauce. She handed out the ingredients – butter, flour , milk and cheese – and began to show the class what they were to do. After she had mixed all the ingredients, the class were sent back to try what they had seen. Mrs Johnston wandered around the room checking that everyone was doing it properly. When her back was turned Billy Watson picked a large spoon, filled it with flour and flicked it towards Tom. It landed on the table in front of him. Tom turned to check that Mrs Johnston wasn't looking and did the same back to Watson.

Before long Mrs Johnston turned to witness the flour fight that had grown in the corner of the room.

"Boys stop that at once!" she ordered. The floor was a mess. There was flour in everyone's hair and all over their clothes. Flour all over the cookers. Flour all over the tables. Mrs Johnston marched angrily over to the four boys.

"Who started this?" the teacher questioned.

No-one answered. The boys all stared at the floor.

"You will all clean this up and see me after school!"

Tom looked at David who shrugged his shoulders they were all going to be punished unless someone confessed. Billy Watson suddenly said:

"It was Tom, Mrs Johnston, he started it."

Tom said nothing and continued to look at the floor.

"Right!" said Mrs Johnston. "Tom, I want to see you at the break."

The boys spent the rest of the class cleaning up the mess and left as quietly as they could when the bell rang. Tom went back to see Mrs Johnston at the break, who gave him a lecture on the standards she expected in her class before giving him a hundred lines on safety in the cooking class.

Creepers

Tom stuffed the punishment in the bottom of his bag and sulked. As he walked to his next class he passed the toilets and was surprised to see water flowing out of the room. The door was slightly ajar and Tom could see Steve Simpson frantically fiddling in the sinks.

At that moment the janitor came running down the corridor. He pushed Tom aside and ran into the toilet. He turned the water off and grabbed Steve. Tom stood against the wall and watched as the janitor shouted to Steve Simpson that he was going to the headmaster. Steve was wailing.

"But the water, I couldn't turn it off!"

Tom laughed. The two made a comical sight marching to the head's office. His hundred lines didn't feel so bad now that he had seen that.

After school, Tom avoided the house and went straight to the well to do his lines. He knew he would get into trouble if Mom saw him doing them. He sat down beside the well and dutifully wrote his punishment. After fifty lines his hand had begun to get sore.

Tom stopped what he was doing and leaned over the well. He thought for a moment about Billy Watson and then placing his chin on the side of the well he said:

The Wishing Well

"Billy Watson is a big pig, I wish I could get even with him."

He looked down in to the dark well, thought about Steve Simpson and laughed.

Chapter 9:

A Troublesome Incident

Mr Watson's garden was his pride and joy. He had entered his prize roses and vegetables in the Rosewell village show for the last seven years and the trophies he had won held pride of place in their living room. It was only when Billy had reached the grand old age of twelve that his father had allowed him to make extra pocket money by helping out in the garden.

Billy had several chores that he was responsible for. Carefully weeding the flower beds, hosing the greenhouse, (and if he was really careful hosing the garden too), and collecting rubbish that had been thrown in by careless passers-by. If he managed to do these tasks without damaging anything that his father cherished, then he could earn an extra five pounds. In the past two years, he had only had one really major accident, when he pulled out one of his father's best roses the day before the annual show. His father's reaction had made Billy very, very careful in the future.

Today was no exception. Billy leapt out of bed

The Wishing Well

and slid into his jeans. It had not been raining for the last couple of days and his dad had mentioned to him the night before that his precious roses would need to be watered. So Billy had pulled his old wellingtons out of the downstairs cupboard in readiness for the watering extravaganza.

The old hose was connected to a tap on the side of the kitchen wall and Billy checked that it was securely fastened on before entering the greenhouse to find the nozzle. The greenhouse held a mixture of flowering pot plants of all shapes and sizes. The varying shades and assorted aromas often made Billy feel warm inside.

Billy placed the nozzle outside the greenhouse, closed the door and walked back to the tap. As he returned he had the strangest feeling that he was being watched or followed. He turned around quickly. There was no-one there. He shrugged his shoulders and carried on down the path.

Anyone watching Billy would have seen a very strange sight indeed, because every time that he walked on, the garden hose shot up into the air and danced behind him down the path like a snake dancing with a snake charmer, and every time that Billy turned round the hose would lie flat on the ground.

Creepers

Billy's hair had begun to stand up on his neck. He really couldn't understand what on earth was going on, but he still had that feeling that he was not alone. Eventually he reached the tap and he turned it on. At the same time the hose danced and slinked its way up to his head height. When Billy turned around he got the biggest fright of his life as he was sprayed full in the face with ice cold water.

"AAAARGH!" he screamed. "What's goin' on?"

He pushed his hands out in front of him to try and see through the blast of water that was drenching him, but the force was too strong. He tried to dash out of the way but the water followed him.

Billy caught sight of the end of the hose as it wriggled and slinked around him.

"What?! Eh?!" he spluttered as the water entered his mouth. He began to panic and started frantically to push the hose away from him as it began to wrap itself around him like a boa constrictor. He fell over and crashed into the flower beds. He heard the snap as the fragile stems of his father's roses cracked around him. There was a sharp pain in his side as the thorns from the flowers tore through his T-shirt.

Billy scrambled to his feet as quickly as he could when he realized what he had landed on, but the plight of the roses soon left his mind as the hose jigged menacingly in front of him. He started to run for the house but the hose barred his way, speedily wrapped itself around his ankles and, with a sharp tug, threw him to the floor. Billy fell on top of another flower bed, mangling himself amongst the thorns. He began to scream.

The screams from the garden caught the attention of his father who had been doing the crossword in his morning paper. Billy's father walked over to the kitchen window just at the exact moment that Billy had foolishly decided to run for shelter to the greenhouse. What his father then saw was his fourteen-year-old son running amok amongst his prize flowers, doing the strangest dance, and crashing into the plant pots. Mr Watson was normally a reasonable man – one who prided himself on his rational behaviour. When he witnessed this display of what his brain told him was wanton vandalism, his mouth fell open and his face looked very pale. He raced out into the garden yelling:

"BILLY, BILLY HAVE YOU LOST YOUR MIND?" Billy was screaming so loud with fear that he didn't even hear his father. What his brain did register though was his father grabbing him to stop him cavorting about. There was a moment of silence. Both father and son stared at each other. The only sound that broke the silence was the trickle of water as it came out of the hose. All around them were broken pots, flowers with no heads on them, large mounds of waterlogged earth.

Billy began to shake and cry. He shakily pointed to the offending hose and through sobs tried to explain to his father what had happened. Billy's father's face turned into a thunderstorm.

"I have never heard such nonsense in my life," he hissed at his son. He marched back to the house to turn off the tap. Billy followed sheepishly behind him repeating:

"Honest dad, honest."

Mr Watson turned around and stared at him, shaking his head and walked into the house. Billy began to follow him still trying to explain when his father slammed the door in his face. Billy heard the key turn in the back door. A loud cry was heard as Billy wailed:

"DAAAADD!"

Chapter 10:

An Old Tale

When Tom arrived at school on the following Monday after Billy's accident, the word had already spread around the school. Some of the boys thought this was hilarious. Billy had apparently got into such a state that he had had to be taken to the doctor. Meanwhile, Steve Simpson had gained a reputation for flooding buildings. He had flooded the toilets in the local cinema that weekend.

Tom sat open-mouthed as David explained to him what he had heard. For a moment he thought about what he had said to the wishing well, then he shook his head. It was just an amazing coincidence.

Neither Billy nor Steve were anywhere to be seen. The school day went without incident due to the absence of the two bullies, although Tom had seen George Foster kicking a can in the playing field and looking a bit lost without his two friends. Tom was settling in much better and was making friends. David told him some more about the haunted forest.

"Well", said David excitedly, "it seems that centuries ago an old witches coven used to meet up in a section of the forest and hold meetings. When one of the local children had gone missing, the villagers went to seek revenge one night and they lay in wait in the forest." David's eyes widened as he prepared to tell the creepy story. "There was a full moon and the witches lit a huge fire and danced drunkenly around it; when suddenly the villagers leapt out and attacked them. There was a huge fight and apparently they drowned some of the old hags in a water well that was nearby."

At his last words Tom gasped:

"A well?"

"Yes," said David, pausing for a large breath so that he could add to the drama. "Some say that soon after, mysterious events happened in that part of the forest. People started to go missing, and some folk said that you could still see the witches dancing around the fire when there was a full moon, so the local villagers boarded it up." David then put on a ridiculous comedy-witch voice and cackled: "An' the well's ne'er been seen since dearie, hahahaha!"

Tom spurted out the words: "But I've seen the well, and it's not boarded up at all. In fact it still works."

"Yeah sure," said David, "it's just a silly tale."

"No, David honestly, I can show you it." David

looked bemused, and as the bell rang they agreed to meet up so that Tom could show him where the well was. Tom decided not to tell David about what he had said into the well – this was all too strange.

After school David came home with Tom. This was the first time that Tom had taken anyone home and Mom was delighted. Too delighted.

"Well Tom, who's this?"

Tom muttered, "David."

"Hello David." Mom had the silliest grin on her face. "And where do you live?"

David bashfully gave Mom his address almost as if she were the police.

"And do your parents know that you're over here?" Mom queried. "It's quite a long way from your home, we don't want them to worry."

As David had rushed home with Tom in excitement he hadn't done anything as boring as telling his parents where he was. Once Mom had grilled him she insisted that he phone them immediately. Tom was very embarrassed.

As Tom suspected, Mom would not be content with David phoning his parents and leaving it at that, she would want to talk to them. She took the phone off David and her voice changed as she attempted to sound posh to his parents.

Creepers

"Oh I'm so pleased to talk to the parents of a friend of Tom's. We're new in the area and I do so like to know the families that are around us."

Behind Mom's back Tom looked at David and pretended to be sick.

"Perhaps we could have David for dinner," Mom babbled on.

Tom smirked at the thought of he and his parents eating David for dinner.

After what seemed like an eternity, Mom put the phone down. She turned around triumphantly, as though she had just solved an important case for the police. Tom sighed.

"Can we go out now Mom?"

"Yes dear but don't go far away, I want to be able to find you easily. I don't want David's parents thinking that I haven't looked after him properly."

Tom and David escaped the clutches of Mom and ran outside.

"Sorry about that," Tom said.

"It's alright," said David, "my Mom is just as daft." Both the boys laughed and began to walk along the path.

When they reached the edge of the forest, Tom was surprised to find that the entrance he usually went through appeared to be more overgrown. The

The Wishing Well

boys pulled away at the foliage until it was easy to climb through. The large field that was sheltered by the trees seemed darker than usual.

Tom looked over to the far end where the well was. "That's strange," he said.

"What?" David seemed amused, "I knew you were lying," and he pushed at Tom playfully.

The boys walked across the overgrown field and arrived at an old boarded up well. The shiny L-shaped handle that Tom had seen before was replaced by a rusty old piece of wire. There was what was left of an old rope hanging from it. The huge well was covered in very old wood that looked rotten and unsafe.

At the side of the well there lay an old bucket with a huge hole in it. Tom was stunned. The stone walls of the well were covered in moss and ivy that had obviously been there a long time.

"But, I don't understand," stammered Tom. "It's not normally like this, someone must have been here." He realized the stupidity of what he was saying as he said it. David laughed loudly. Tom was confused.

"Yeah," said David mockingly, "someone came along and made everything all rusty and stuck the ivy on the side. Don't be ridiculous Tom, this well hasn't been used for years." David tried to turn the handle, it wouldn't budge.

"Maybe those stories are true. What about the witches?" Tom looked pleadingly into his friend's eyes.

"Oh Tom please," laughed David, "you're making my sides hurt." His laugh echoed around the large field. "C'mon, let's go back, I'm cold and hungry."

They walked back to the farmhouse with David making fun of Tom all the way. Tom was far too stunned to defend himself.

When David left that evening he was still chuckling at Tom, and he thanked him for the best laugh he had had in ages. Tom was taking it well but as he closed the front door behind him he thought:

"Straight after school tomorrow I'm going back to the well."

Chapter 11:

Tom Makes a Wish

The day seemed to drag as Tom impatiently waited for the last bell. Steve and Billy had returned and had teamed back up with George to bully a boy in first year. Tom avoided them and hoped they had forgotten all about him. Besides, he had more important things to think about. He got into trouble in several classes for daydreaming but he couldn't stop thinking about what had happened.

Eventually the day finished and he set off for the bus. He had managed to get to the bus stop without any incident because Steve and George had been absent, and he kept his fingers crossed that today would be the same.

He hurried along the canal path with the well on his mind, not noticing the three boys who followed alongside in the bushes.

Just as he reached the bridge the boys pounced on him. Tom struggled to get away but George Foster grabbed his bag and began to run in the opposite direction from the bridge.

"Give that back!" he shouted after him.

Foster laughed and mimicked his voice: "Give that back!"

Tom tried to get to his feet but Simpson and Walker pinned him to the ground. George began to swing Tom's bag round and round by the strap. Some of his books fell out onto the muddy path. With one last fling, George threw the bag into the canal. It landed with a splash and lay in the middle of the water. Tom could see his chemistry book sticking out as it became waterlogged. The other two boys let him go, but jeered and made rude gestures as they all ran off.

Tom waded into the water to get his things. He picked up the books that had fallen on the path. Everything was covered in mud and water. From the knees down his trousers felt cold, damp and heavy. He looked up the path to where the boys had gone and saw them laughing and play-fighting as they headed off.

He walked over the bridge, leaving a soggy trail. His trousers had begun to smell. He had missed his bus and took his place in the queue. People wrinkled their noses and looked around to see where the smell was coming from. Tom's face reddened. Eventually the bus arrived and he clambered on and quickly went to the rear, trying to hide his legs under the

The Wishing Well

seat in front in the hope that would reduce the smell.

Unfortunately Tom had sat beside the bus radiator and the heat began to warm up his trousers. Steam started to rise off them and the smell soon took over the whole vehicle. Tom pressed his face up against the window so he would not see the look on the other passengers' faces.

He got off the bus as quickly as he could. The change of temperature from the warm bus made him shiver. He was angry.

The bottoms of his trousers had become stiff and he waddled towards his house.

Mom was outside beating a rug when he arrived.

"Tom!" she shrieked. "What on earth. . .?"

Tom looked at her sheepishly.

"Do you think I have nothing better to do than wash clothes every day?" she asked sharply.

"Sorry Mom, I fell in the canal."

Mom sent him straight upstairs to get a bath, delaying his visit to the well. Tom fumed.

After they had dinner the telephone rang. It was Aunt Margaret.

Tom knew that this would mean his mother's attention would be occupied for a while and he took the chance to slip out of the house. It was beginning to get dark but Tom hardly noticed as he ran down the now-familiar path to the edge of the forest.

When he got there he couldn't see the broken bushes that he and David had pushed aside yesterday. It looked exactly the same as it always did. Tom looked around to see if a tractor had been by to take the bushes away, but there were no tracks. Only his own footprints in the mud. He slowly edged into the field, feeling a little bit nervous. He could see the faint glow of the low evening sun glimmering at the far end of the field. It seemed to light up the well – almost as if the well was on stage and standing in the spotlight. Tom ran over to the well and stared.

It was as he suspected. The well looked exactly as it had done the very first time that he'd discovered it. The handle shone brightly as the sun's rays bounced off it. The rope was attached strongly to the shiny new pail. There was no sign of any old boards or a rusty old bucket with a hole in it. He leant over the side and shouted into it.

"Where have you been?!"

The well echoed his words. Tom scratched his head in amazement – this was the haunted well and the spirits of the dead witches lay in here. He thought about Steve and Billy and didn't feel frightened by the well at all. It was his friend. Then he remembered George throwing his schoolbag into

The Wishing Well

the canal and a mischievous thought crossed his mind.

If this was truly the haunted well then perhaps the spirits had been responsible for the accidents that the boys had been having. It was time to do an experiment.

"Spirit of the well, I hate George Foster" he said excitedly "I wish, I wish that he could feel the way I did today and worse."

The well murmured back the last echoes of his words. Tom stood very quietly and stared inside. He noticed that the sun had all but disappeared now and the meadow was almost fully dark. He ran back to the house laughing, impatient to see if his wish would come true.

Chapter 12:

George's Lesson

George Foster wasn't the brightest boy in the world. He had a habit of saying the wrong thing at the wrong time, and in general he was a little slow. Steve Simpson allowed him to hang around because he was too stupid to think about what he was doing and would do whatever he was told. Steve had told George to throw Tom's bag in the canal and George hadn't thought about the consequences of this. He had just done exactly what Steve had told him to.

Today was no different from any other day for George. He had gone home for his tea and was now in the back garden throwing stones at the cat. The cat tried to dodge the missiles but George had the poor animal trapped in the corner. He grinned stupidly to himself as the cat mewed in distress.

The back door of his kitchen opened and a disembodied voice shouted:

"George, stop that." The door closed as quickly as it had opened.

George looked up at the door and for a second was confused. His Mom always stopped his fun.

The Wishing Well

What did she care, it wasn't their cat. He reluctantly let the cat go and began to kick a can about the garden.

He noticed something in the ground in the corner of the garden. He hadn't seen that before, what was it? It was a large square drain that stuck up from the earth. Why had he never noticed that before? He had explored every inch of this territory. The drain had a barred grate that covered it. George peered inside and he could see that it was a deep and dark hole. He knelt down beside it and listened. It sounded like there was water running through it.

He looked around the garden for something to prise off the metal grate. Beside the shed lay the handle of an old rake. George picked up the handle and forced it between the bars. He heaved his body on top of the handle and the grate began to shift. George chuckled to himself. The grate loosened and he was able to slip his fingers into the earth around it. He pulled hard and it swung towards him like a gate.

George leaned over and listened hard. There was definitely water running. He picked up the can that he had been kicking around earlier and dropped it into the drain. It disappeared from view and George leant over to hear it drop. Suddenly a great force sucked him into the drain. George tumbled head first down the hole but his trouser belt caught in the opening and he stuck halfway in.

He wriggled about to try and loosen himself and stuck even tighter. His legs were sticking straight up in the air. George began to shout "HELP!" but his cries were swallowed downwards into the drain. It was dark and damp and had a very unpleasant smell. George thought he recognized the smell but couldn't quite remember where he'd smelt it before.

At that moment a familiar sound came from George's house. It was the sound of someone in the bathroom flushing the toilet. George opened his mouth to call out again, when he heard the sound of rushing water getting louder and louder and nearer and nearer. He began to wriggle furiously but it just made things worse. He was well and truly stuck.

The water was rushing towards him like a volcano erupting and he remembered where he knew that smell from.

This was the drain connected to the toilet. George began to scream frantically as the water gushed all over him. He didn't think to keep his mouth closed and he gurgled the word "HELP" swallowing an enormous amount of sewage as he did so. The water shot up his nose and the smell was unbearable.

The Wishing Well

George's mother thought he had been very quiet in the garden for a while and looked out of the kitchen window to see if he was still there. What she saw was the dreadful sight of George's legs wriggling out of the ground. She threw open the back door and screamed "George, oh NO!" She ran towards him and tried to pull him out of the drain by the legs. There was water everywhere and she slipped on the paving stones and landed on George with a thud sending him skooshing down into the sewer.

"George!" she screamed into the drain. George's cries could be heard getting further and further away.

"MUUUMMM! HEELLPP!"

Mrs Foster ran back to the house and phoned the fire brigade.

Chapter 13:
The Spirit of the Well

By the time that Tom arrived at school the next morning the news had spread like wildfire. It had taken four hours to track George down in the sewer. When they recovered him he had had to be taken to the hospital to have his stomach pumped as he had swallowed so much sewage. Tom was delighted. It had worked, so the well *was* haunted.

When he got home that night he didn't even go into the house. He ran straight to the well, unable to contain his excitement. It looked as it always did for him, but now it really was his special place. He had decided after David's visit not to mention it to anyone else.

Tom ran into the field leaping and whooping. He spun round and round until he fell in a heap in front of the well. He began to laugh and laugh. He hung over the side and shouted:

"Thank you, thank you spirit of the well."

Tom laughed until his sides hurt. He lay down on the ground beside the well and looked up at the tree-hidden sky above him. It was then he noticed

The Wishing Well

how quiet it was here. He could not hear a bird or the wind rustling through the leaves of the trees. The sky seemed to darken as he sat up and looked around the field.

There was not a sound to be heard. Tom looked at the well which seemed to give off a strange glow. A mixture of colours swirled out and around it. Tom stared at the well, rooted to the spot. Gold, green, blue and red seemed to spin together like a tornado. Whirling around the well until they became a large blanket shape. Tom's jaw fell open. Suddenly the shape formed into a large cloak that appeared to be wrapped around someone or something.

Tom stood in front of the vision and stared in disbelief. The cloak opened up and revealed what it had been hiding; a small ghost-like creature that hovered above the ground. The creature had long black hair that blew around it, despite the fact that there was no wind. It wore a long flowing gown that was made of a material that he had never seen before. It seemed to change in front of his eyes. Sometimes it was ice blue, then it seemed to blend into purple and magically it drained into deep midnight blue.

Tom stammered "Wh-who are you? Are you the spirit of the well?" The creature threw its head back and laughed a long and hollow laugh that seemed to last an age. The sound of its voice was strange. It seemed to be mixed with a watery sound as though it was drowning as it spoke. The laugh echoed around the field and eventually died away.

"Tom, we meet at last." The creature spoke slowly and flashed its green eyes at him. Each time it said a word its eyes seemed to glow even brighter. "I am indeed the spirit of the well, I have waited a long time to be released, and at last someone has said the words to break the spell that held me prisoner in my watery cell."

The sound of the spirit's voice made Tom feel heady, enchanted by the vision. He could not speak.

"Fear not young Tom," bubbled the spirit, "for you have proved that we have a common goal. I too have enemies against whom I long to seek revenge. Three times you asked me to do your bidding and three times I obeyed. You broke the spell by thanking me for my evil doing."

Tom found the power of his voice.

"Who cast a spell on you?"

The spirit's face contorted. It bubbled and spat out the words.

"The local people of Rosewell. They accused me of being a witch," the spirit's eyes flashed and

The Wishing Well

narrowed with anger." They came for me like cowards in the night. Hiding in the bushes while my sisters and I danced in the moonlight. They set upon us, murdering my beloved sisters. I tried to escape but they captured me and threw me to my death down this well." The spirit let out an unearthly wail.

"Why are you not dead then?" Tom asked.

"Aah!" gurgled the spirit. "I am the undead. As I fell to my death I was caught by a stronger power. Enki the goddess of the waterworld captured me and softened my fall. She was not happy with what I had been doing while I was alive – she took the side of the villagers and punished me. She said I must repent my beliefs and then she would allow me to rest in peace, but I would not, for my name is Spite, and I would not agree to her terms. She was wrong to judge me so." The spirit writhed around, changing in hue and hissing and spitting.

"My punishment was to remain trapped in the well until another human followed my way of thinking. Which is what you, dear, dear Tom have done." Spite smiled at him revealing bubbles that spurted out between her teeth. "Three times you must ask for my help, three times I must do your bidding, then you must thank me and you did. Now I can right the wrong that has been done to me and then and only then can I join the souls of my sisters."

"But surely that was centuries ago, the people that you want must be dead," said Tom.

The spirit screamed out aloud:

"NO, NO, I WILL NOT BELIEVE IT!"

Tom looked nervous – he had obviously said the wrong thing.

The spirit spat out the words "I WILL HAVE MY DAY, I WILL HAVE MY REVENGE! NO-ONE WILL STOP ME!" It spun wildly around until its tornado reappeared, then just as mysteriously as it had appeared, it vanished. Tom stood still, mesmerized by what he had seen. This was truly amazing.

It was still quiet in the meadow and he crept over to the well and looked inside. There was nothing there, nothing to see. Where had she gone? He picked up his bag and ran back to the farmhouse.

Chapter 14:

The Water Queen

Tom sat in his bedroom. He was meant to be doing his homework but he couldn't concentrate. Perhaps he had imagined what he had seen, but it all seemed so real. If it was real then Spite was a force to be reckoned with. She seemed very angry – very angry indeed. He wondered when he would see her again. He needed to find out what she intended to do. The people she wanted revenge against were well and truly buried. His heart filled with dread at the thought of what he had released.

That night he couldn't sleep. He tossed and turned in his bed. Spite was in his dreams, wreaking havoc wherever she went. He woke up and looked at the clock. It was half past four in the morning. The room was cold and dark and he pulled his covers tightly around him and tried to keep the heat in the bed. Suddenly there was noise at the window. Something was tapping on the glass, Tom ran over and pulled the curtains back. Spite hovered in front of him.

"Let me in Tom," she hissed, "let me in."

Creepers

Tom unlocked the window and the spirit flew in. The dark room became a rainbow. Spite's eyes flashed at him.

"Get dressed Tom , we have work to do."

Tom looked at the clock and tried to say,"But it's only four thirty, I have to go to school in the..." Spite interrupted him sharply.

"I've waited a long time for this." Her green eyes flashed with impatience. Her mouth seemed to bubble furiously. "There are people who need to be dealt with and I don't like to be kept waiting."

Tom got the distinct impression that now was not the time to argue. He quickly pulled on his clothes while the spirit hovered in the corner of the room. He walked towards the door.

The spirit spoke: "We don't have time for your conventional way of travel – come to me." She beckoned to him and Tom nervously walked into her arms.

Spite enveloped him in her cloak. Tom could smell an aroma of weeds and dampness. The embrace was not cold but neither was it warm. She lifted him up into the air. He couldn't see the ground but he knew he was no longer standing on it.

Spite propelled them out of the window and they soared high into the sky. The night was clear and the

The Wishing Well

stars sparkled above them. They seemed to swoop and dive with incredible speed, until eventually they landed. Spite opened her arms to reveal the front of the village pub, The Traveller's Arms.

Tom couldn't work out why they were here. Spite looked down at him and laughed at the curious expression on his face.

"This, Tom, is where it all began," she said – her eyes twinkling in the dark night. "I need you to help me as there are some things that I cannot do."

The pub had an old sign showing that it had been there since 1850. Spite pointed to it.

"You mocked me when we had our earlier conversation but this ale house still stands,"

Tom tried to tell her that the pub would have a different manager by now, but she had begun to make her way to the back of the building.

Outside the building were large empty metal barrels that were waiting to be collected in the morning. Spite hovered above them and beckoned to Tom.

"Climb up on these and open the window up there."

She pointed to a small window that looked like it might be the toilet.

Tom looked at her and said:

Creepers

"I can't do that, I'll get into trouble. Spite, this is wrong."

The spirit puffed up her cheeks and blew them out straight in Tom's direction. What came out of her mouth was a mixture of water and weeds. Tom was drenched from head to foot.

"Do not incur my wrath or I will not be responsible for the outcome."

Tom climbed up on the barrels and pulled at the window. It was not locked properly and swung open, showing the darkened bathroom. Spite flew in over his head. Tom decided to follow her and climbed in. The spirit flew into the main bar and hovered menacingly.

"At last, I return!" She spun in the middle of the room and her cloak filled it with light. She began to spin faster and faster while reciting the words:

"Absence makes the heart grow fonder,
Broken sleep gives time to ponder.
While apart, time I've not wasted,
My true wrath remains untasted.
Here within this drinking inn
Bring the waterworld within.
Soak them, drench them as I have been
A legacy of the Water Queen!"

The Wishing Well

Tom stood in the corner of the room watching the display. Spite spun around the room like a top, reciting the words faster and faster. There was a rumbling noise and cracks began to appear across the ceiling. Loud bangs began to come from the bathroom behind him. Tom looked in the bathroom to see water shooting upwards from the sinks. The pipes on the walls began to groan and bend until they burst. Water cascaded from the room. The bottles in the bar began to smash and water ran in from the roof. Spite was laughing and her voice echoed around the room.

A voice came from upstairs. The landlord lived above the pub and had been awoken by the crashing and banging that was happening around him.

"WHO'S DOWN THERE!"

Tom looked at Spite who was still spinning and pointing at various places were new rivers of liquid would appear. There was the sound of feet on the stairs and Tom called out to her:

"Spite, we must go!"

She spun over in Tom's direction and without stopping wrapped him in her cloak and whirled through into the bathroom and out of the window. They rocketed into the sky leaving the watery mess behind them. As quickly as they had reached the

Creepers

village, the spirit returned Tom to his bedroom, landing him in the middle of his room. Tom stood looking bedraggled, still wet from the soaking that she had given him for questioning her. Spite placed a watery finger under his chin and said, "There now, wasn't that fun?"

Tom was still thinking about the soaking and decided to agree with her – he nodded.

"I am tired now. I think I need a little rest. All that hard work has made me weary. I must go."

With that final comment she disappeared through the open window leaving Tom staring after her, cold, wet and very, very worried.

Chapter 15:

Spite Seeks Revenge

It was the weekend and Tom had spent the last few days thinking about nothing else but Spite. There had been a report in the local paper that said vandals had broken into the Traveller's Arms. Tom felt very guilty and worried that he was responsible. Spite hadn't been back to see him since that night and he was hoping that that would be the end of her revenge and that she was now at peace with her sisters. He had not dared to visit the well since the flooding but Mom and Dad were going into town and Tom thought that this would be his opportunity to try and summon Spite. He had to be sure that she had returned to rest.

He waited a while after his parents had left to be sure that they had definitely gone and wouldn't return. As soon as he felt they must be far enough away he walked down to the well. He wasn't sure what to expect when he got there. Perhaps it had gone back to its rundown state which would mean that Spite had gone. He entered the field cautiously and stood staring at the well. It was in perfect condition. The sun shone on the chromed handle and the shiny pail swung securely on the rope.

"Hmm," thought Tom, "I'm going to have to try and summon her."

He leant over the side of the well and shouted:

"Spite, are you there? I need to talk to you." There was no answer. He tried again.

"Spite, it's Tom, I need to talk to you." He thought he heard a faint giggle and he leant further into the well and listened carefully. "Spite, is that you?" Tom felt a tap on his shoulder and he jumped.

It was Spite – she was hovering behind him.

"Boo!" she said, and then she laughed. "Did I frighten you – am I scary?" She lifted up her arms, dancing around like a ghost and rolled her eyes around in their sockets. "I've been practicing my haunting – what do you think?"

Tom was glad to see that she had a sense of humour and laughed. Maybe she was going to be good after all.

"Spite, we need to talk," Tom sounded quite serious, "please listen to me."

Spite gave him a look, as though he was spoiling all her fun.

"Oh all right," she pouted, "if you insist. What is it?" Spite seemed to stop rippling in the air and remained still for a change.

Tom began to explain that what they did the other day was wrong and that the people responsible for her sisters' and her death must surely be dead as it was over a hundred years ago. Spite said nothing. Tom looked at her face to see if she was getting annoyed – he didn't want her to drench him again. She appeared calm so he continued. He asked her if she was now satisfied and would she be happy to return to the well? Spite put on the most innocent look and said:

"Tom, you're absolutely right, I understand, but there is one more thing I need to do before I can join my sisters, will you help me?"

Tom wasn't sure.

"It depends on what it is, we can't inflict any more damage."

Spite nodded and said:

"No, I just have to look up an old friend."

Tom thought about it for a second then looked at Spite's face.

She looked like she truly meant it and it might mean that the problem of having released her would be solved.

"Ok", he said, "I'll do one thing; but promise me there will be no trouble." Spite nodded obediently and opened her cloak to enclose him in it.

Within seconds they were winging their way through the skies. Spite was singing a song to herself and Tom hoped she remembered that she had him with her. He covered his nose to try and lessen the smell of dampness that came off her and prayed that this would not be too long a journey. They soon arrived at the back of the local freezer shop in the village. It was lunchtime and there was no-one to be seen. Spite seemed slightly confused as she looked around.

"This is where John the blacksmith used to work. But this does not look like his place."

Tom felt exasperated with her.

"That's what I've been trying to tell you! The people that hurt you are no longer alive."

Spite's eyes flashed in frustration. She looked as though she was thinking hard.

"Well never mind, this will do just as well. Come, Tom, you must help me."

Tom felt nervous when she said this to him. Last time he had helped her they had caused an awful lot of damage. Spite was looking at the back doors where the food was delivered for the freezers. It was a large steel one and Tom didn't see how they would get inside. He was relieved.

The Wishing Well

The spirit turned and looked at him.

"Tom, I need you to open this door."

Tom told her that he couldn't and that the shop was shut. Spite began to look angry. She puffed up her cheeks.

"OK," said Tom. He hadn't forgotten the horrible damp smell of the last time she puffed up her cheeks at him. It had taken him three washes to get the smell out of his hair. He walked around the outside of the building to see if there was any other way to get in. High up on the first floor, a window was open. He turned to Spite and showed her. She lifted him up and hovered outside the window. Tom was getting used to being held up in the air by her. He prised the window open further and Spite followed him in.

Once inside, Spite weaved her way through the corridor and down the stairs as she went to the main shopping area. They were soon in the large hall. A sea of freezers stood humming before them. Tom walked down the aisle looking into each glass chamber. There was ice cream, burgers, chips – all sorts of things. He normally hated coming here with Mom but it was different being here with Spite when no-one else was there. Spite scooted up and down the aisles until she found a place that she was comfortable with. She then began to spin.

Tom turned around quickly and shouted at her:

"Spite, remember you promised!"

There was a long hollow laugh as she cried in return:

"I lied!"

The spirit spun wildly and viciously around and Tom cringed as he heard her begin to recite the words of her wicked spell:

> "World of ice, that replaces what I knew
> Frozen spite returns to you.
> Melt away the years of pain
> So I can love my own again.
> Bring me water, water clear
> From every pipe and tap that's near.
> Show this town that I've returned
> Never again to be spurned!"

Tom felt the floor beneath his feet begin to shake uncontrollably.

"No Spite! No!" he cried.

The spirit ignored him and continued to recite the words as she spun faster and faster in a blur. In the midst of which Tom could just catch sight of her eyes flashing at the utterance of her words. The building shook and tiles from the ceiling began to fall. There were large groaning noises as the pipes in the building that held water began to burst above Tom's head. The hum of the freezers had stopped and their lids flew upwards. Water began to gush out of the machines.

Tom ran toward Spite to try and grab hold of her and stop her spinning but there was nothing to hold on to. His hands disappeared through her shape as though she didn't exist.

The spirit spun feverishly around and soon her laughing replaced the incantation that she had used to destroy the shop. There was water everywhere and Tom's trainers were beginning to become waterlogged. A steady stream of water gushed from the ceiling soaking his hair and clothes.

"Stop, Spite stop!" Tom cried in vain as the evil spirit got exactly what she wanted.

Tom began to run out of the food hall towards the stairs that they had come down. The spirit screeched at him.

"Get back here!"

But he didn't listen and he kept running until he reached the next floor. Spite was behind him and she pointed her water hand at the ceiling above his head. The tiles above him fell at his feet and water poured all over him. Tom kept on running. When he reached the store room with the window that they had climbed into he realized that he could not get out. He was going to have to go back the way that he had come and get out through the fire escape. He turned quickly and looked out of the doorway. There was no sign of Spite. Where had she gone? The water had now flooded the whole building and Tom sploshed his way back down the stairs trying to be as quiet as he could so that she wouldn't hear him. The sound of rushing water was deafening as he waded his way to the back corridor. A voice stopped him in his tracks.

"And where do you think you're going?" Tom knew who it was without looking. He turned slowly to face the monster he had released from the well. Spite hovered above him with the strangest expression on her face. "I haven't finished with you yet."

Tom began to run towards the door and the spirit pointed at him firing missiles of water. One hit Tom in the middle of his back. He fell over sprawling in the watery mess.

"No, Spite no!" he cried. He knew that he had to get out of there and he launched himself at the bar which opened the door. The sea of water behind him

The Wishing Well

followed him out into the delivery yard.

Tom sailed out the door on a wave of water and landed on the ground outside.

Not stopping to think, he leapt up and began to run as fast as he could, away from the disaster.

Chapter 16:
Out of Control

Tom had run all the way back to the farmhouse looking behind him constantly to see if Spite was following him. His clothes were cold and wet and stuck to his skin. When he got back he was relieved to see that Mom and Dad had not returned yet. He ran upstairs and pulled off his wet clothes. He quickly changed into dry ones and locked himself in his bedroom. His mind raced with the memory of what had happened. This was terrible, Spite was out of control. Who could he tell? How could he stop her? He heard a thud downstairs and his heart skipped a beat. Had she come to get him?

"Tom, are you here?"

It was Mom. He let out a sigh of relief. Tom unlocked the door and ran to the top of the stairs, but what met him was not the familiar face of Mom – it was Spite. She hovered at the bottom of the stairs laughing. Tom ran into the bathroom and locked the door. He knew she couldn't get into rooms unless the door was left open. He must have left the front door open. How could she copy Mom's voice? Spite

The Wishing Well

had come to the top of the stairs and was mimicking Mom's voice again.

"Tom," she crooned, "come to Mommy!"

Tom put his hands over his ears and shouted "Go away, go away!"

Spite's laughter echoed around the empty house and Tom tried his hardest not to hear her. She began to chant:

> "Little boy that's good as gold,
> Always does what he is told,
> Released the spirit from the well
> Liked it fine when his foes he felled."

Tom could see lights flashing under the bathroom door as Spite began to spin.

> "Let's teach him not to mess with fire
> Water always cools that pyre.
> Bring him trouble, the water kind
> Something that will blow his mind."

With that, she let out an unearthly cackling laugh. Tom looked around the room and realized for the first time where he was. He was in the bathroom. He leapt to his feet and grabbed all the towels he could find. The rumbling had begun. Frantically he looked at where it came from. The toilet had begun to bubble and froth. Tom quickly pushed as many towels as he could down the bowl. He turned to the sink and tried to tighten the faucet as much as he could.

It came off in his hands sending a fountain of water high into the air. The toilet had begun to seep water around the towels and the bath began to gurgle and burp as though it had just eaten a very large meal. Water oozed everywhere.

Tom was rushing around the room mopping up as much water as he could but the room quickly became drenched. Suddenly there was a furious knocking on the door.

"Tom," said a sharp voice "Are you in there? Open this door at once!"

Tom shouted, "Go away I hate you!"

There was a brief silence from outside the door and then a very angry voice spoke:

"Thomas Walker, open this door right now." It was Dad. Tom looked around him at the mess and knew that he was in deep trouble. He opened the door and stared into Mom's and Dad's angry faces. Mom looked past him into the room and let out a shriek:

The Wishing Well

"HAVE YOU LOST YOUR MIND?"

Tom said nothing. What could he say that didn't sound silly? His parents pushed past him and slopped across the bathroom floor. Mom lifted her towels out of the toilet.

"My good towels, I don't believe this!"

Tom couldn't remember the last time that he had seen both of them so angry. Dad told him to go to his room. He did it quickly without arguing – now might not be a good time to discuss anything with them.

He closed his bedroom door quietly behind him and sat down on the side of the bed. He was going to have to stop Spite.

Mom and Dad did not speak to Tom for the next two days. They made him help to clean up the mess and said nothing to him – they just gave him the occasional dirty look. Tom felt terrible but what could he do?

As they sat down to have tea one night, Tom could bear the silent treatment no longer. He decided to tell them what had happened. Mom and Dad sat perfectly still and listened to what Tom said without interrupting. Tom looked from face to face to try and gauge what they were thinking, neither parent spoke.

Creepers

"Honest Mom, Dad, I'm telling you the truth. Come to the well and see," he pleaded with them. The two parents looked at each other. Mom's eyebrow was raised.

"OK," said Dad, "we'll do just that." Tom felt relieved.

As they walked along the path toward the forest Tom chatted excitedly to his parents about the spirit. Mom and Dad still said nothing. They got to the edge of the forest and Tom noticed that the hedgerow had grown back again. He and Dad hacked their way through the overgrown bush and then climbed through. The field was quiet and again the sun peeked through the tree tops and lit the meadow. Tom ran over to the well and stopped dead in front of it. His parents walked slowly behind him and they all three stared.

They were staring at an old disused boarded-up well. It had a rusty old handle and a broken piece of rope hanging from it. On the ground lay an old pail that had a hole in it. Tom turned to his parents in despair.

"I know what it looks like, but I told you it looked like this when I brought David here, you've got to believe me!"

Tom's Mom looked at his dad and said "That's it

The Wishing Well

Arthur, I'm calling the doctor as soon as we get back to the house."

Dad nodded at her. "I think this time you're right Phyllis," he replied calmly.

"NO! I'm telling the truth!"

Tom shouted at them but his parents just looked at him sympathetically.

"Tom, it's the move – it's been more stressful for you than we imagined."

Tom knew that his arguing was in vain. He walked behind them to the edge of the field with his head down. Just as they climbed through the gap in the trees he thought he heard someone laughing – he turned back to look but there was no-one there.

Chapter 17:

A Helpful Priest

The doctor arrived that evening and sat in the living room with Tom's parents. Tom sat on the stairs, trying to hear what they were saying – after all, it was about him. Eventually, after what seemed like ages, the door opened and Tom's Mom called him in. The doctor was a large jolly-looking man who appeared to be having a problem keeping a straight face.

"Come in Tom," he chuckled. "Sit down. Now, what's all this I've been hearing?"

Tom decided not to tell the doctor what he had told his parents and instead he shrugged his shoulders. The doctor gave him a checkup, taking his temperature and listening to his chest. "Even if I was mad listening to my chest wouldn't help," Tom thought. After at least half an hour, he announced his diagnosis to Tom's family.

"It's stress. Try not to let him get too excited," and with that he left.

Tom looked up at his parents who looked very concerned. Maybe they were right, maybe he had imagined it all. Mom told him not to go back to the well again and Tom agreed.

The next day was Sunday and the Walkers went to church. Tom sat through the service and looked around bored. This was his first time in the local church since they had moved here. After the sermon, Mom was talking to the priest and Tom saw them looking at him with worried expressions. Mom came over and suggested that Tom might like to talk to Father Stephen who was interested in Tom's story. Tom looked at the ground and shuffled his feet.

When everyone had gone, Tom was left sitting in the pew at the back of the church. Father Stephen came and sat beside him. He was a rather stout man with a soft voice. He began to ask Tom questions about the last place where Tom had lived. Tom answered dutifully but felt uncomfortable. Father Stephen then said the strangest thing.

"I've lived here a long time Tom, and I've seen many strange things."

Tom looked up at him, unsure about what he was trying to say. Father Stephen continued.

"I think I've got something that might interest you, come with me."

The old priest stood up and held his hand out in the direction they were going. Tom followed him to a small vestry at the back of the church. The priest began to take off his robes and offered Tom a seat.

"I've got a strange story to tell you," the priest began. "When I was new to Rosewell the people here were quite set in their ways. This is an old village with a great deal of local history. Some people call them old wives' tales and some say they're fact."

Tom was interested – did the priest know the story of the well?

"Ah," the priest smiled kindly at him, "now, the story of the well has had many versions over the years. Some say the woman who was drowned was a witch and that she threw herself down the well to escape her pursuers. I've also heard that she threw herself down the well because she had a broken heart, but one thing that is true is that a woman drowned in that well. Whether she was a witch or not, we'll never know."

Tom looked into the priest's face and decided that he could trust him. He told him what he had seen. The old man was silent for a while as he pondered over the tale that he had just heard. He stood up and walked across the room to a bookcase which contained many large, old books.

"When I came here Tom, these books had been here for a very long time. Some of them are journals that the local priest at that time kept. I think this one in particular might interest you"

The priest laid the enormous book on a large table and switched on an overhead lamp that lit the yellowing pages underneath. Tom and Father Stephen leant over the book. The writing it contained was very old and fancy. Tom could only make out certain words, and some of the words had faded with age. Father Stephen fumbled around inside his jacket and produced a pair of glasses which he perched on the end of his nose.

"D'you see here Tom?" he pointed to a scrawl at the bottom of the page. "That signature there says Father Pettigrew, and right next to that it has a date, can you read that?"

Tom screwed up his eyes and managed to pick out the date 1887.

"Now that," whispered the priest, "was Father Pettigrew's last entry. If we go back a few pages he's got something quite interesting to say."

The old man and the boy pored over the tome and together they managed to pick out the details of the lynching that took place in the forest that terrible night. Father Pettigrew had recorded the meetings that the villagers had to plan the attack on the witches. He had written down the names of the three

Creepers

women: Spite, Malice and Vengeance. The three sisters had come from a home that had a history of black magic and the villagers had easily come to the conclusion that the women were responsible for the disappearance of some children. The book also told where the women had lived: under the barn that stood opposite Tom's house. The priest looked at the boy and said, "I think that old barn might be worth a visit."

Chapter 18:

The Mystery of the Barn

Father Stephen came round to the house that afternoon. He sat with Tom's parents for a while, sipping tea and eating cake. Tom sat on the edge of his seat, desperate for the priest to come with him and explore. When Tom was convinced they couldn't possibly eat and drink any more, the adults proceeded to do so. Tom was exasperated. Eventually the priest stood up.

"Ah, there's nothing like a good cup of tea Mrs Walker."

Mom smiled, her best smile for guests, and walked the priest to the door. Tom thought Father Stephen had forgotten what he'd come here for and then the priest turned to him.

"Tom, will you walk me to the end of the lane?"

Tom nodded, perhaps a little too eagerly, and Mom gave him the strangest look.

They walked out into the courtyard and crossed to the barn. The Walkers didn't really use the barn, they had just stored some old furniture in it. Tom pulled open the rickety door. The priest and the boy walked in. The barn smelt odd and had various hooks and ropes that hung from the beams high above.

"I remember the family that lived here before," Father Stephen looked around. "They used to keep horses in here. See – over there you can still see where the stalls for tying up the horses used to be."

Tom looked over to where the wooden walls were marked. The ground of the barn was covered in stone slabs strewn with hay. Father Stephen began to push some of the hay aside and Tom noticed that there were some stones that were darker than others. The priest stood still and stared down at the ground.

"It's as I suspected," he said gravely. Tom looked at him, confused.

"Help me clear the floor."

They pushed as much of the straw away as they could. It became clear that there was something drawn on the floor. At first it looked like a child had drawn something on the ground but then it became clear. There before them was a large circle. Within the circle was various symbols of animals that had human heads.

"What is it?" Tom asked the priest.

"That," said Father Stephen, "is what's keeping your spirit of the well with us. It's an ancient druid's circle for summoning people back from the dead."

The Wishing Well

Tom looked aghast and felt the back of his neck start to prickle.

"I think we can use this to get rid of your spirit once and for all," said the priest. Father Stephen explained no more but got into his car and left for the church. He told Tom that he would phone him and reminded him to keep away from the well.

Tom could hardly sleep that night for two reasons. One was that the spirit might come and visit him again and the other was wondering what Father Stephen was going to do. He did feel a lot better knowing that the priest believed him and was going to help. The night passed without incident and Tom was disappointed to wake in the morning and have to go to school.

That day was a long one. He couldn't concentrate in his classes and his mind was on other things all day. He said nothing to David, who had forgotten all about his visit to the well, which pleased Tom as he didn't want to talk to him about it. The three bullies had been keeping a low profile since the spirit of the well had visited them. So Tom's day passed without bumping into them. When the school day finally finished Tom got ready to catch the bus with butterflies in his stomach.

As he came out of the school he was surprised

Creepers

to see Father Stephen waiting for him. The priest beckoned him over.

"Tonight Tom, I'll meet you at the barn at 7 o'clock."

Tom began to ask what the priest had in mind but he just repeated "tonight". Tom's bus journey home gave him time to wonder what on earth was going to happen tonight.

Chapter 19:

A Spell Goes Wrong

After dinner, Tom sat at the living room window staring at the barn. It was only 6 o'clock and the next hour was going to take forever. He turned to stare at the clock on the mantelpiece when he thought it must be seven o'clock but only fifteen minutes had passed.

"Tom go to your room, you're making me jumpy," his Mom had scolded him. Tom went immediately so that Mom didn't force any information out of him.

At last, Tom heard the sound of the car in the drive. He was here. He ran downstairs and out of the front door, crashing straight into Father Stephen who was carrying a large bag. The priest placed his finger over his lips and then pointed at the barn. Once inside, the Father pulled out the large book that belonged to Father Pettigrew from his bag.

"Look at what I found here," he said, and turned to the back of the book.

There was a drawing of a circle exactly the same as the one that they had found on the floor of the barn. On the outside of the circle stood three items:

a pail, a bottle of water and a thick piece of rope.

"What does it all mean?" asked Tom.

Father Stephen began to read the writing that was underneath.

"It would seem that Father Pettigrew had been forced to summon up the water spirit to try and rid the village of her, and this is how he did it. He placed the pail, with some holy water in it, and a thick piece of rope in the middle of this circle and recited these words that are written here."

Tom read the short spell that was written there. It looked like the sort of thing that Spite would say herself.

There were four short lines and then the page was ripped off.

"Where is the rest of it?" Tom asked. The priest said he couldn't find them. They then set about doing what Father Pettigrew had done. Tom found an old pail. Father Stephen pulled out a bottle containing water that he said he had taken from the font in the church and poured it into the pail.

"What about the rope?" asked Tom. The priest rooted in his bag again and pulled out a thick piece of rope.

"It's a piece I cut off one of the bells in the tower – it's for a good cause." His eyes twinkled at Tom and

The Wishing Well

he placed it in the circle. Once the pail and the rope were in position, the two of them looked carefully at the spell. Father Stephen made the sign of the cross and then began to recite in a clear loud voice:

> "Circle of evil, hear my spell,
> Recreate the water well.
> Show the hideaway so rich,
> That conceals the water witch."

Tom looked around the barn for a sign that the spell had worked. Absolutely nothing happened. The priest repeated the spell again. Again nothing happened. Tom stood beside him and looked at the notebook again – there had to be something that they were not doing. They both read the page again.

"What if something important is on the bit of paper that's missing?" Tom queried. The priest shrugged his shoulders. Then, Tom noticed something at the top of the page that was almost faded away.

"Look, there – it looks like it's a sign for raining." Father Stephen screwed up his eyes in the dimming light.

"Ah" he said triumphantly, "I know what that is." He marched over the circle and headed straight for the pail. With the bottle he had brought he scooped out some of the water. "Now Tom, I have to sprinkle the holy water over the circle whilst you recite the spell."

The priest began to do just that. Tom said the words carefully and kept his eyes on Father Stephen at the same time. He kept repeating the words until the father had walked completely around the circle. When he reached Tom there was a flash of light. Tom and Father Stephen stared at the centre of the circle. Tom saw what he'd seen the first time that he had met Spite. A mass of interwoven hues that seemed to swell up into a giant sheet. The priest's mouth fell open as he watched in awe. Greens, golds, blues and reds knitted together in a whirlwind. When they stopped spinning, Tom was surprised to see that Spite was not in front of him – the well was. It looked brand new and untouched. The pail was shiny, the rope white as the first day it was hung and the handle was shiny and free of rust. Tom began to walk towards the well.

"No Tom," said the priest, "stay beside me." Tom turned to look at Father Stephen's face and decided to stay. There was another flash of light and the whirlwind began again. This time, Tom knew that Spite was coming. He could hear her roaring with

The Wishing Well

anger as she was forced to appear at someone else's request.

A tornado spun violently around until the huge cloaked figure appeared.

The spirit hovered in front of them with her cloak shielding her face.

"What do you want?" she hissed.

Neither Tom nor the priest answered.

"Well?" she shouted and peeked through the folds of her cloak. On seeing the priest she screamed. "Aagh, I hate holy men!" She buried her face further into the cloak. Father Stephen raised his cross and pointed it at her.

"Return to where you belong!"

Spite spun full circle and seemed to go quiet and limp. Then she began to giggle. "I've met your type before. Do you honestly think that feeble command will work on me?"

Father Stephen repeated his words. Spite spun high into the air, then dived head first into the well and disappeared. Tom and the priest stared at each other. Had it worked? There was total silence.

Suddenly there was the sound of rushing water and the well began to rumble and froth.

Spite shot out of the well like a cannonball that had been fired from its barrel. She was laughing and her eyes were flashing.

"There's going to be trouble now," she cackled at them and remaining high in the air she opened her mouth and spat a long missile of fluid at them.

They both ducked but the force of the missile hitting the barn wall made the building shake. The spirit began to swoop and dive like a bomber as she aimed water missiles at them. The priest held out his hand and grabbed Tom as they both made a run for the door.

"Going somewhere?" spat the spirit as she fired another torpedo of sewage at them.

"Run, Tom, run!" said Father Stephen and the two of them headed out into the courtyard and ran for cover.

Father Stephen began to fumble in his jacket for the keys to his car. Spite spat at him just missing his head and splattered water all over the windshield. The priest managed to get the door open and leapt in a second before another missile was launched at him and hit the closing door of the car. He put his lights on to try and see Tom. He could just make out the corner of his shirt as the boy hid behind an old horse trough. He started up the engine of the car and headed over towards him. The spirit was spinning madly above the car and screeching at the top of her

The Wishing Well

voice. Father Stephen managed to spin the car in front of Tom and opened the door to let him in. Tom jumped in and the priest pushed his foot down on the accelerator and sped off towards the village.

Spite began to blow water on the road. Once the water made contact with the concrete, it became a sheet of ice in front of the car causing it to skid from side to side.

"We must have done the spell wrong" Tom shouted at the priest. The father said nothing as he tried to keep the car steady on its course. The water missiles that missed the road landed on the car and sheets of ice covered the glass. Father Stephen turned on his windscreen wipers and tried to blow the screen clear with the heater.

Tom could see Spite hovering above them through the sun roof of the car. She spat and twisted as she chased the car towards the church.

"We'll be safe in here," the priest nodded as he pulled up at the back of the building. They leapt out of the car and ran to the vestry at the back of the church. They ran into the small study and slammed the door shut. Father Stephen locked the door saying, "Just in case." The pair of them sat down and thought about what had happened.

"There must be something else we can do," said

Creepers

Tom. Father Stephen began to pace up and down the room rubbing his chin as he thought.

"The only thing I can think of is that we must have missed a bit of the spell out."

He walked over to the bookcase and began to pull the books out onto the floor. He was mumbling to himself as he opened the odd one and quickly flicked through it.

"No, not this one," he murmured and would grab at another one. Tom asked if he could help. What were they looking for?

"Anything, anything at all that looks like it might help."

They poured over the journals searching frantically for any information. Then, just as Tom was handing one of the books back to the priest, a couple of sheets of paper fell onto the floor. Tom picked them up and read what was on them.

"Father, it's the rest of the spell!" he shouted. The priest clambered over to him and read the pieces of paper.

"Aha, we've got to get back to the barn." He stood up and helped Tom to his feet. "C'mon lad, we've got work to do."

Chapter 20:
A Final Showdown

They crept around the outside of the church, looking above their heads at all times to be sure they were not being followed. When they reached the car Tom reached over to open the door. As he pulled on the handle the force of something on the other side pushed the door towards him. He fell back onto the priest as water poured out of the car. Spite had flooded it.

They climbed in and squelched into the chairs. The seats were completely waterlogged. The smell in the car reminded Tom of the first time that Spite had wrapped him in her cloak. It was a damp and musty smell, almost the same smell from the local canal. He pressed his face into his hands so that he wouldn't have to smell it.

They slowly drove out of the church driveway. When they reached the large pillars that opened onto the road there was a sudden flash of light, which nearly blinded both of them. It was the spirit. She hovered in front of them barring their way. Her eyes flashed bright green, her clothes changed from purple to icy blue. Water and weeds bubbled and frothed from her mouth as she gurgled with delight. She had captured them. Tom suddenly remembered the time that he had tried to grab hold of her.

"Drive, Father Stephen, just drive, we can go right through her." The priest pushed his foot onto the pedal on the floor and the back wheels spun as the car picked up speed and shot through the archway. It lurched into a sea of mist as it became entangled in her cloak.

"Keep going!" Tom shouted and the priest carried on, bursting through the veil.

They landed on the road outside the church and the wheels screeched the car round into the wide street. Father Stephen began to drive as fast as he could in the direction of the farm. Spite was chasing behind them, hurling her missiles in their path. The icy blankets spread across the road forcing the car to spin round in a circle. The priest struggled with the steering wheel and managed to get control of the car once more.

Again, they headed for the farm. There was a thud on the roof of the car and the shape of two footprints pushed through, banging the side of Tom's head. The car swerved across the road, the brakes squealing as Father Stephen tried to control it. A large sheet of ice

The Wishing Well

was ahead of them and the car turned onto its side slipping off the road and colliding with a tree.

For a second Tom was stunned. Where was he? What was happening? He suddenly remembered and looked over at Father Stephen. He leant across him to see if he was alright. The old man opened his eyes.

"It's all right Tom, I'm okay but I think my leg's broken." Tom looked down to see the front of the car squashing his leg.

"Take this," said the Father and he pulled out the words of the spell. "Go to the barn – follow the instructions – Go! GO!"

Tom grabbed the pieces of paper and stuffed them into his jacket pocket. The crash had jammed the car door and he had to kick it open.

He still had about a mile to go to reach his house. He was going to have to avoid Spite. He began to run up the dark road. There were no street lights as they were outside the town. Tom kept turning around and looking above him to see whether Spite was there. There was no sign of her. He reached a clump of trees and stopped to get his breath back. He leant on the tree with his hand on his side as he panted. He felt a bead of sweat running down his forehead, he wiped it off. As he took his hand past his nose he caught a whiff of the damp odour that went with Spite. He slowly looked above him and there she was grinning. The sweat hadn't been his at all – it was her. The spirit placed herself in the middle of the road. She puffed out her cheeks and blew. A large jet of water hurtled towards Tom, knocking him off his feet. He skidded into the road, ripping his jeans.

He could hear Spite's cackle behind him. He picked himself up – his knee stung – and then continued running. The spirit danced around him blowing him this way and that as though he were a feather. He kept falling over and then picking himself up. He realized that he was near the farmhouse and he began to run in a zig-zag so that it was hard for her to hit him. He reached the barn ran in and closed the door.

The magic circle remained clear as it had before they had managed to summon Spite. In the middle sat the pail with the holy water and the rope. Tom picked up the empty bottle and filled it from the pail. He then sprinkled the holy water over the circle. He picked up Father Pettigrew's journal, placed the missing pieces of paper together and began to recite the spell:

The Wishing Well

"Circle of evil, hear my spell,
Recreate the water well.
Show the hideaway so rich,
That conceals the water witch.
Spite so evil needs to rest,
In the real world she's a pest
Take away her water powers
Lay her to rest among the flowers."

There was a loud rumble and a haze began to dance around in front of Tom's eyes. There seemed to be a mass of lights and the well appeared. Tom stood still and under his breath he repeated the spell again. The whirlwind began. Tom kept catching glimpses of Spite in amongst the tornado.

"No! NO! I'm not finished!" she screamed, and her voice became tinier and tinier as she seemed to disappear down a long tunnel. There was a large sucking noise almost as though a huge vacuum cleaner had been switched on and the whole vision disappeared right in front of Tom's eyes. There was total silence.

Tom remembered Father Stephen and ran over to the house. Mom and Dad were sitting in the living room in front of the television. They did not look round when he came in. They had heard and seen nothing. He went into the hall and phoned an ambulance and told them where the accident had been. Tom went into the kitchen and found a flashlight. He ran out of the back door towards the forest. The flashlight lit clumps of the wood as he ran down the path. When he got to the entrance of the wood the bushes had become overgrown again. He pulled back the spiky hedgerows and climbed into the meadow.

He walked slowly over to the well, his heart beating quickly. When he got there he stood still and stared. There in front of him was an old boarded-up well. It had wooden slats bolted across the large water hole. It had a rusty old handle that hadn't been used in years. A threadbare rope hung from the middle of the beam, clearly showing that at one time it had held a bucket. There on the ground was a rusty old pail with a large hole in it. Tom leaned against the old well and smiled.

Also Available

BEGGAR BOY

Tommy and his mom move to a new house and all their neighbors seem to be better off than them. The other kids from the area take great pleasure in picking on Tommy and always remind him how poor he and his mom are. Tommy then gets help from a curious lad that seems to appear when he needs a friend. With his new friend, he takes revenge on the snobbish kids around him. But where did this mysterious friend come from? And why is he helping Tommy?

GHOST WRITER

Charlie is a schoolboy with a talent for writing but even he cannot remember writing all the words that appear in his note book. There seems to be a story being told on the pages of his note book but who is doing the telling? Charlie's headmaster is showing just a little too much interest in the note book and does not seem very happy with Charlie. Ever been scared of your headmaster? I mean REALLY scared!

MIRROR MIRROR

The Johnstone family buy an old mirror. Soon, the children of the household think they can see an image of a girl trapped inside it. She is dressed in strange clothes and seems to be trying to communicate with the children. What is the mysterious story of the girl? And why is she trapped in the mirror?

THE PIANO

The Houston family appear to have found a great bargain when they buy a beautiful piano for a really low price. However, the piano seems to have a mind of its own. In fact, no matter what tune people try to play on it, the piano wants to play its own haunting music. What is the piano trying to tell the world? And have the Houstons got more than they bargained for?

THE SCARECROW

In the countryside, people often become attached to the land that they are born on – but a scarecrow? Mysterious happenings on the Davis land make young David too curious for his own good. But the more he investigates, the more he wishes that he'd kept his mouth shut. And so does the scarecrow!

THE GHOSTLY SOLDIER

Angus and Isobel love to hear the stories about heroic Scottish warriors. They visit the site where the Battle of Culloden was fought and Angus romanticizes the events, wishing that he could have been there to help fight the Redcoats. His opinion changes when an explosion in their garden unleashes the spirits of the English and Scottish soldiers who must fight the battle again and again. The children must return the spirits to where they belong. But how?

Also Available

BLOOD ON TAP

Bill Todd is delighted to have found a new house for his family. It's cheap, in a good neighborhood and it will provide much-needed space for his growing family. His wife and his young children – Alex, Beth, Gary and Karen – are not so sure. The house looks sinister and feels even more creepy. They all have a very bad feeling about it, but Mr Todd will not change his mind. Number 13 Blackday Avenue is just what it appears to be, and very soon they encounter something that makes them wish they had never moved.

DOCTOR DEATH

Have you ever gone to the doctor with a minor illness only to find that you feel even worse? That's what happens to Josh Stevens and his friends. They turn from a bunch of healthy kinds into smelly, greasy, pustulent wrecks – and coincidentally they have just paid a visit to the charming and handsome Doctor Blair. Josh's hideous boils are jeopardizing a future date with the lovely Karen but there are much more sinister "remedies" luring in the good doctor's medicine cabinet. But how can Josh and his friends stop Doctor Death carrying out his deadly plan?

EDGAR ESCAPES

After bringing many other ghostly and despicable tales to your notice I decided that I must tell my own story. Confronted with this demand for knowledge, I felt it was only correct that I should submit my story to you. Dear reader, I would not be anything without your attention. I will reveal the person behind the stories, where I am from, just how I tell my tales from behind the grave and the deadly purpose I have. Now, I ask you to read on – if you dare!

SOUL HARVEST

The Grimaldis, a creepy new family who have a bad attitude and who dress in black move into Billy and Alice's neighborhood. Very soon afterwards their Mom and Dad and all the other neighbors start to act very strangely – as if they have suddenly become wicked. The children, and their friends Ricky and Alex, are soon the only normal ones left in a neighborhood of thieves, bullies and thugs. The entire village, headed by the Grimaldis, are soon trying to find the four children and capture their souls to make the imminent "harvest" complete!

HAPPY HALLOWEEN

Samantha, James and Mandy are brother and sisters. Their parents decide to take a break in a quiet village the weekend of Halloween. The children are rather concerned that staying in a boring village is going to spoil their trick-or-treating. Halloween is certainly going to be very different to usual – but it will be far from boring! Samantha discovers an old spell book and that she alone is capable of harnessing its dangerous powers. She is soon drawn into a sinister and terrifying world of wizards and witches and must escape or lose her life and risk the safety of the normal world.